CONTENTS

Heart *of* Britain

BOOKMAN
PUBLISHERS

Heart *of* Britain

ISBN 1898718 52 0

First published 1996 by
Bookman Publishers
Floor 22
1 Canada Square
Canary Wharf
London E14 5AP

1 2 3 4 5 6 7 8 9

Designed by Associated Design Consultants
Scanning and Image Quality: John Symonds

FOREWORD

Heart disease, the biggest killer in the Western world today, still claims one in three lives and many readers of this book may have lost family members and friends this way.

I have been privileged to see for myself the miracles – at the very leading edge of medicine today – performed by the teams of surgeons, doctors and nurses at Royal Brompton Hospital, whose dedication saves so many lives.

I have been profoundly impressed, too, to see how bravely patients cope, and have been particularly touched by the courage and trust shown by Britain's little people – our children. All need our compassion, our love and our support at what is often their darkest hour.

This book, *Heart of Britain*, has been made possible by people across the whole of the country who took part in a photographic competition to raise funds to help children and adults suffering from heart disease.

As the Millennium draws near and a new age dawns, let us hope further research at Royal Brompton will bring to mankind increased knowledge of the causes of heart disease, new treatments, less suffering and, perhaps most important of all, understanding and compassion for those in need.

Diana, Princess of Wales

SPONSORS & SUPPORTERS

This book would not exist without the help of the companies and people mentioned on this page

Dixons

Official Sponsor
TOMORROW'S BRITAIN

Official Sponsor
CARING BRITAIN

SUPPORTERS OF HEART OF BRITAIN:

AMV Group, BP, Halifax Building Society, Hillsdown Holdings, JCK Holdings (UK) Ltd., Marks & Spencer, Mirror Group

Olympus Cameras, who donated Mju-1 cameras as prizes for each section winner .

Fuji Cameras, who donated DLT75 cameras for use by the celebrity supporters.

ACKNOWLEDGMENTS

The Publishers would like to thank the following people for their invaluable help in creating this book:

Royal Brompton Hospital:
Sir Phillip Otton, Bill Bain, Mark Taylor, Professor Anthony Newman Taylor, Susanna Hammond, Averil Slade, Edel McCaffrey, Valerie Fone.

Heart of Britain Office:
Sir Harry Solomon, Maurice Lazarus, Anna Khanova, Sabine Kahn, Janie Joel.

The Insight Group:
Colin Harper and Fiona Brooks.

Mirror Group:
Roger Eastoe, Jill Palmer, Sharon Collins, Helen Reilly, Mike Maloney, Kent Gavin, Nick Fullagar, Maureen Sayers, John Rolls.

Associated Design Consultants:
Bob Searles, Ian Murray, Sue Spurling, Jan Leeks, Gareth Parkinson, Martin Barfoot, Andrew Thomas.

Practical Photography Magazine:
Martyn Moore and David Corfield.

Fotorama:
Alan Williamson.

Alison McDougall for taking many of the pictures of celebrities for Chapter 10.

Also: Frank Gill, Cherry Hughes, Deanna Maclaren, Ann Miller, Rik de Stroumillo.
Special thanks to Mr Mohamed Al Fayed, Chairman, Harrods Ltd.
And the people of Britain who responded so warmly and wonderfully to the Heart of Britain Campaign.

THE HEART OF ROYAL BROMPTON HOSPITAL

ROYAL BROMPTON HOSPITAL, renowned worldwide for its pioneering medical advances in heart and lung disease, treats patients from across the entire UK, from Europe and beyond. It has the expertise, the tools, the scientists and the doctors to save lives.

Heart and lung disease together remain the UK's biggest killer, and few families across Britain have escaped its clutches. The *Heart of Britain* campaign has been set up to raise funds to change this harsh reality and enable Royal Brompton to play its part in reducing the numbers afflicted.

Dame Margaret and I have been fortunate to have participated in some of the leading-edge medical advances pioneered here. Within the past few years, dramatic improvements have taken place arising from research in the treatment of heart and lung disease – advances which only 10 years ago we would never have dreamed possible.

By purchasing this book you will be playing *your* part in our fight to prevent heart and lung disease.

Projects to be funded from the money raised by *Heart of Britain* include:

- A special catheter laboratory, enabling children to have high-tech treatments without the need for major, painful, open heart surgery.

- The development of our artificial heart programme. 4000 people a year need transplants but a shortage of donor organs means that only some 400 each year actually receive a new heart.

- The use of gene therapy to treat people suffering from the inherited disease cystic fibrosis.

One of the most fulfiling experiences for all of us – whether doctor, relative or friend – is to see a desperately ill patient return to health and happiness. And when our research teams find solutions that could save thousands of lives, that too will be magnificent.

Thank you everyone – our sponsors, the people across the nation who sent in their pictures and the patients who allowed us to photograph them to help publicise the campaign. Special thanks must also go to Diana, Princess of Wales, for her sustained support throughout the campaign and for her ongoing care and compassion for those in need.

Professor Sir Magdi Yacoub – Professor Dame Margaret Turner-Warwick

JUDGING DAY AT CANARY WHARF

From left to right, Nick Kent, Terry O'Neill, Trevor Leighton, Brian Aris,
Bert Kwouk, Mike Maloney FRPS, Kos Evans, Vince Hill, David Corfield, John Stoddart,
Bob Searles, Annie Hill, June Brown and Brian Moody.

THE JUDGES

Our grateful thanks go to the team of judges who had the difficult task
of choosing the final pictures for this book from the many thousands submitted.

THE STORY OF THE BOOK

It was a chilly week for the time of year, and on the surface, everything seemed normal. England was mourning the Euro football triumph that might have been, but at Wimbledon spirits rose as "Tiger" Tim Henman kept British hopes alive to the quarter finals. And on Men's Final day, it was a streaker who took the glory. Pilots were threatening to ruin everyone's summer hols by going on strike, and Northern Ireland was on the boil again.

But in one very special way it was a far from ordinary week. All over the country, thousands of people with cameras were making history.

The first week of July 1996 was Heart of Britain Week, when men, women and children nationwide took photographs summing up the Heart of Britain and sent them in to a competition raising funds for Royal Brompton Hospital's Appeal to boost research into heart and lung disease.

On August 19, a team of expert judges and celebrities made their final, agonisingly difficult choice from the tens of thousands of pictures sent in. The winning photographs make up the major part of this unique and fascinating book, *Heart of Britain*, from which all royalties go to the Royal Brompton Appeal.

As you will see, life just bursts out of the pages. Laughter, sorrow, hope and despair are there for all to see. In the nine categories from Beautiful Britain to Tomorrow's Britain, ordinary people and experienced photographers captured the soul of our nation as we approach the Millennium. Taken as a whole, the book provides a stunningly honest record of the way we are, and how we feel about our country and ourselves.

We have included two extra chapters: The Heart of the Heart of Britain is a photographic record of the campaign itself, the famous people who supported it so well and the events that put it on the map. Then there is a chapter devoted to the work of the professional photographers who helped the campaign.

To everyone who made the Heart of Britain campaign the great success it has been, I thank you - from the heart.

Nick Kent
Publisher, London, August 1996

THE WINNING PICTURE

STEAM RALLY BOY

Mr A L Douglas
Long Eaton
Nottingham

SECTION WINNER

Poppies

IAN D MACFADYEN

Godalming, Surrey

Beautiful
Britain

CHAPTER ONE

Benbecula stag
NEIL ADAMS
Balloch, Scotland

The open sea
JOHN BAKER
Dovercourt, Essex

A scene from Gloucester docks
JEFF WILSON
Gloucester

Lligwy Bay, Anglesey
MRS B BARNETT
Cossall, Nottinghamshire

Drystone walls in Swaledale, N Yorks
ANON

Sunset
DAVID BLACKMAN-WELLS
Littlehampton, Sussex

Rape at Bamburgh
M DAVIDSON
Southwell, Nottinghamshire

Bude harbour
GRAHAM WARREN
Sanderstead, Surrey

The gym hut in Glen Kinglas
LISA PALFREYMAN
Letham, Angus

Poppy fields
Peter Walker
Kingswinford, W Midlands

Mowcop Castle, Cheshire
Mark Bourne
Shelton, Staffordshire

Tower Bridge at night
LES HUNT
Benfleet, Essex

Message from space
LISA PALFREYMAN
Letham, Angus

**Lucy & Alice in the Heart of
Britain**
MR J RACK
Northampton

Midsummer night's dream
KAREN TEAGLE
Furzton, Milton Keynes

Reflections
MRS M ROBINSON
Wootton, Northamptonshire

I believe in working my way up
MR MYLES
Cannock, Staffordshire

Morning mist at St Andrews
ALAN ESPLIN
Weybridge, Surrey

In the distance
MARGARET GOULD
Davyhulme, Manchester

Rannoch Moor

ELIZABETH HODGE
Craigend, Glasgow

Berkeley Castle

PAM GASTON
Gloucester

Shadowland
MISS SALLY MARSHALL
Herongate, Essex

Crummock reflections
J RAISBECK
Egremont, Cumbria

**Early morning, Loch Etive,
Argyll, Scotland**
MRS A L HOPPER
Alnwick, Northumberland

Scott monument at dusk
ANDREW R HENDERSON
Edinburgh

COVER
IMAGE
WINNER

Worth waiting for
Ms Vivienne Chick
London

Calm after the storm
FRED STOCKING
Wroughton, Wiltshire

Ballerina and chorus (London)
CLIVE B HARRISON
Bracknell, Berkshire

Edinburgh open
D T H ROBERTS
E Croydon, Surrey

Day closes
MRS JUDITH BARNARD
Derrythorpe, N Lincolnshire

The old village pub
Mr M Mulvany
Westcliff on Sea, Essex

**The still of a sound
(in Scotland)**
KATHY SOUTHWELL
Edinburgh

Oban sunset
JAY BERMAN
Manhattan Beach, California, USA

**Dunbar parish church: Royal
British Legion window**
GARRY S MENZIES
East Linton, E Lothian

Overleaf
Rhosneiger, Anglesey
ANON

Padstow harbour
LUCIEN LAVENTURE
London NW8

Patriotic flowers
G Johnson
Felling, Tyne & Wear

North Uist landscape
Neil Adams
Balloch, Scotland

Hippo by the sea

DAVID ALEXANDER BARRIE

Dundee

After the storm, Loch Linnhe

ANON

Tay rush
Andrew Gibb
Perth

Bath
CARMEN BALANZA
London SW11

**Dying embers: the Cutty Sark
at Greenwich**
SIMON PETER JONES
London SE18

First light
MR GERRY BARNARD
Derrythorpe, N Lincolnshire

SECTION WINNER

Sleeping on the job
KERRY TURNER
Irchester, Northamptonshire

Working Britain

CHAPTER TWO

**Tired, after a hard day's
work at the yard**
CLARE HAMMOND

Sorry, out of service
VICKI COUCHMAN
Southsea, Hampshire

Good clean fun
RUSSELL B MARTIN
Wallsend, Tyne & Wear

British beef
Mr A Bailey
Oxford

**Twins Georgia & Katie Rudd,
3 years old**
Mrs Rita Cave
Immingham, N E Lincolnshire

Did you say LEAVES on the line, sonny?
Mrs H M Sulley
Redhill, Nottinghamshire

Trimming the wicket
Mr D L Harding
Tredegar, Gwent

Young artist
Mr D L Harding
Tredegar, Gwent

Two hours to go
MARGARET GOULD
Davyhulme, Manchester

Little boy lost
BRIAN PERKINS
Studley, Warwickshire

At the workface
MRS B FERGUSON
Leicester

**A horse, a horse, my
kingdom for a horse**
ROGER MILLWARD
Sanderstead, Surrey

**The dying art of
thatching in Sussex**
ANON

Lattice on gold
LINDA BANFIELD
Machen, Gwent

Edinburgh

ANON

What fire?

MARK SCOTT

Southport, Lancashire

Can I help?
Mrs C Hughes
Frodsham, Cheshire

**Have a heart mate,
give us a hand**
Roy Bevan
Freshfield, Merseyside

Ready for business
STEVE BRYANT
Grays, Essex

**The Recession pub,
Stratford upon Avon**
CHRISTOPHER SNOWDON

The heart of the city
MARION DAVIES
London NW11

The Royal Lancers
David Payne
Chessington, Surrey

Smiling manikin
Anthony James
London N5

Hello, hello, what
do we have here?
ANON
Gildersome, Leeds

Oyez, oyez
N A DE-PULFORD
Diptford, Devon

Overleaf
Hole in the road, Holland Park
ADRIAN LEGG
London W11

Going up
ROGER MASON
Shrewsbury, Shropshire

Smoked fish
ALAN REID
Edinburgh

Smithy at work
LYNNE WILLIAMSON
Castel, Guernsey

Clocking on
SUSANNAH CLARK
Brentwood, Essex

SECTION WINNER

Alone together

MARK BOURNE

Shelton, Staffordshire

Good Time
Britain

CHAPTER THREE

Night at the kebab house
HELEN REES
Thames Ditton, Surrey

Out of step
LYNN TAIT
Westcliff on Sea, Essex

If they can do it, so can I

CLARE HAMMOND

My family in Lyme Regis
MAISIE HILL
Lyme Regis, Dorset

Variety is the spice of life
Mrs Hilary Hay
Leicester

Wow, it is noisy, Mum!
Tony Swift
Allestree, Derby

Oops!
RACHEL LUM
London NW6

Floating
Marion Davies
London NW11

Smile please!
R V Watts
Chrishall, Hertfordshire

The pecking order
MRS M SMITH
East Barnet, Hertfordshire

Fun at the fair
Tom Unwin
Norwich, Norfolk

Southsea carnival
Trevor Malcolm
Portsmouth, Hampshire

Vamp till ready
JILL FRY
Holbury, Southampton

Firework fantasia
BRIAN PERKINS
Studley, Warwickshire

Little and Large
Mr K Bryan
Liverpool

**Coronation Street and the
ups and downs of life**
Lindsay & Paul Corrick
Radcliffe, Manchester

A step in the right direction
R V Watts
Crishall, Hertfordshire

Jolly good company
LYNDA KEY
Whitestone, Nuneaton

Spot the difference
MR J E BAILEY
Chelmsford, Essex

Be happy
BRIAN HUGHES
St Helens, Merseyside

Beating the heat
ROBIN RACKSTRAW
Chalfont St Giles, Buckinghamshire

I've got no hang ups!
KAYE ANDREWS
Chippenham, Wiltshire

Sweetie
JACKIE E McCORMICK
Marske by Sea, Cleveland

Say cheese
Helen Coxon
Kimberley, Nottinghamshire

Angus – airborne!
N G G Herrtage
London SW18

Summer time blues
CLAIRE MORRIS
Newton Abbot, Devon

My brother's a nobody
TERESA MOODY
Hedworth, Tyne & Wear

Making the most of it
Miss Jane Feagan
London SW20

Overleaf
Boot sale, glorious Devon
Mike Thompson
Paignton, Devon

It's a hard life
MISS EMILY HORNE
Crowborough, E Sussex

Catching the sun
MRS J COMLEY
Dorchester

Lazy day reading
Mr A L Douglas
Long Eaton, Nottinghamshire

Gone fishing
Margaret Gould
Davyhulme, Manchester

Soaking up the atmosphere
ROY BOOTH
Fleet, Hampshire

Heart of pride
GAVIN MCGRATH
Clapham Common, London

Eric Claptout
DEAN FARDELL
Grantham, Lincolnshire

A dancing meringue
Debbie Hoare
London W4

**Let the good times
rock and roll**
CHRIS ALLEN
Winslow, Buckinghamshire

It's no fairy hangover
A J PRINCE
Burnham, Buckinghamshire

Lovely Liverpool lass
SYLVIE MCCARTHY
Liverpool

Having a ball
SALLY MARSHALL
Brentwood, Essex

JOINT SECTION WINNER

I'll get there one day

C P CRITCH

Worsley, Lancashire

Britain

On the Move

CHAPTER FOUR

My Blue Heaven
MR A S TAYLOR
Newhaven, E Sussex

The A12 by night
ANNA CARPENDALE
Capel St Mary, Suffolk

The through train
KERRY TURNER
Irchester, Northamptonshire

But I want a blue one!
JOHN REYNOLDS
Benfleet, Essex

Mission impossible
Clive B Harrison
Bracknell, Berkshire

Red Bus Rover
Jill Cleghorn
Haggerston, London E8

facing page
Caution at the lights
Stanley Allman
Poulton le Fylde, Lancashire

Up, up and away
JON BUNSTON
Southampton, Hampshire

Travelling in style at Henley
LUCY BODEN
London W8

The great leap forward
Liz Ball
Calderstones, Liverpool

"Victory" amphibious vehicle in St Aubin's bay
Mrs Helen A Lisher
St Helier, Jersey

Framed
IAN GOLLINS
Crewe, Cheshire

What next – topless?
MRS P HUGHES
Clubmoor, Liverpool

Gone away (sign in Colchester)
KEITH PRESTON
Saltaire, W Yorkshire

Which way are we going?
MS M WINDROSS
Chatham

Brolley trolley
BERT WHALLEY
Ulverston, Cumbria

Equestrian request
ALEC TAYLOR
Preston, Lancashire

JOINT SECTION WINNER

Tour de Fence

PAUL J C MACKLEWORTH

Melksham, Wiltshire

Royal Yacht Britannia escorting
Queen Mother to Falmouth
PEARL BANNISTER
Priors Marston, Warwickshire

Snowdon mountain railway
Llanberis to summit, centenary
year 1896 – 1996
PAMELA HAIGH, ARPS
Henleaze, Bristol

Call sign "Seabird" alias Concorde.
TERRY HANSON
Cullingworth, W Yorkshire

Mustapha Trip
MR J DAVIES
Birkenhead, Merseyside

Overleaf
Old and new
MRS ANN LYFORD
Watford, Hertfordshire

SECTION WINNER

──────────── ❦ ────────────

Gone, but not forgotten
MR J DAVIES
Birkenhead

Caring **Britain**

CHAPTER FIVE

Is this really the Nineties?
C P CRITCH
Worsley, Lancashire

**Barbeque lunch for
nursing staff**
MR A MORRIS
Worthing, W Sussex

Careful does it
VAL BLEASDALE
Instow, Devon

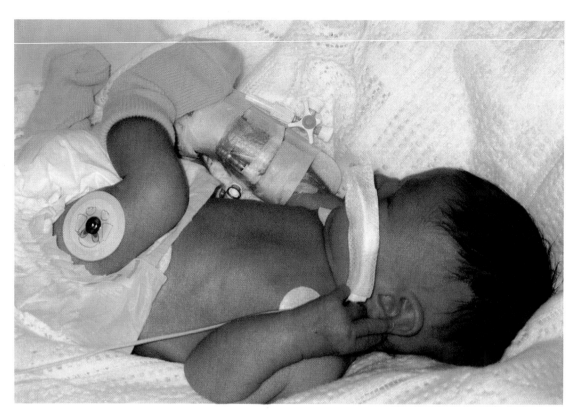

**Willpower – Luke Ansbro,
patient at Royal Brompton**
HELEN JENNINGS
London EC1

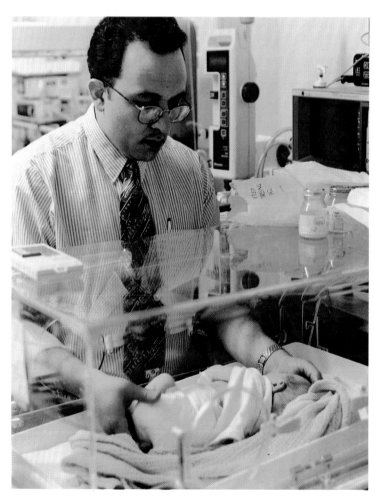

**With loving care at Greenwich
Hospital baby care unit**
J MCMAHON
Plumstead, London SE18

Butlins
Mrs Rose Willamson
Clacton on Sea, Essex

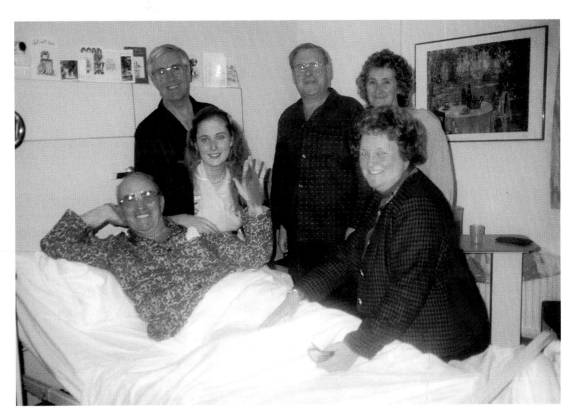

John, four days after his triple by-pass op at Royal Brompton
John Probert
W Pontnewydd, Gwent

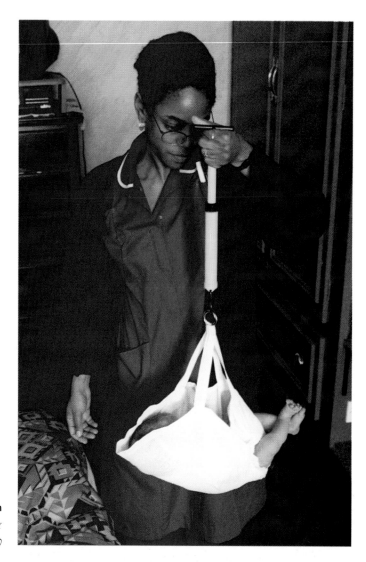

Weigh in
Tim Hoy
Willesden, London NW10

In the nursery, we share
Mrs K Sturges
Sanderstead, Surrey

Hello son,
I'm your Dad
JEAN ENTWISTLE
Staplefield, W Sussex

Cheer's Mum
MR E A F GOODYER MBE
Dartford, Kent

**Preserving Britain
– 238 years old**
MR D A ALLEN
Long Eaton, Nottinghamshire

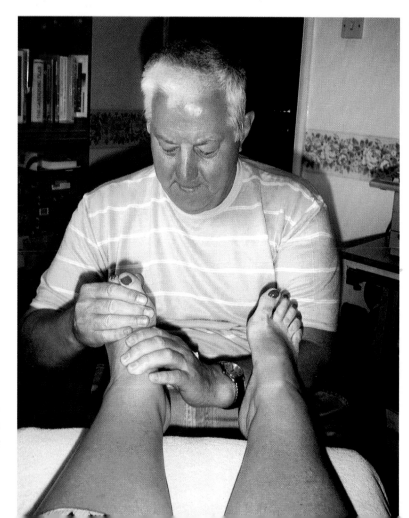

This little piggy…
MRS JACKY EDENBOROUGH
E Goscote, Leicestershire

Where's Mum?

JILL CLEGHORN

Haggerston, London E8

**Right, I'm giving you a hug
– now where's my SWEETS?**

MISS L RYAN

Abington, Northamptonshire

A bird in the hand
GORDON E WILLIAMS
Narborough, Leicestershire

**Move over a bit and
give me a cuddle**
MISS IVY HAWKINS
Stone, Staffordshire

Jump jockeys
CHRISTINA RADMALL
Shoreham, W Sussex

The grand generation gap
MRS J A SHIRLEY
Hatfield, S Yorkshire

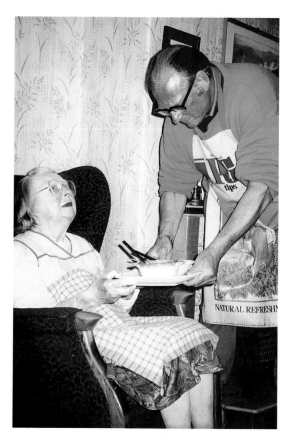

Mam's dinner
MRS SYLVIA WHALLEY
Ulverston, Cumbria

Time out for a chat
CHARMIAN BERRY
Woodbridge, Suffolk

Looking through the years
SIMON WHALLEY
Epping, Essex

SECTION WINNER

Face to face with a frog

JOHN HOWARD

Tealby, Market Rasen

Animal Britain

CHAPTER SIX

Where is that fish?
Mrs L Skelcher
Rosehill, Oxford

"Cats" and dog
J B Whitby
Anstey, Leicestershire

Keep off my patch!
C P Critch
Worsley, Lancashire

Hello, deer!
D COMPTON
Rendcomb, Gloucestershire

"…and then I starred in…"
MR GERRY BARNARD
Scunthorpe, N Lincolnshire

Anyone at home?
JENNY GARDNER
Rainham, Kent

Kingfisher
PETER SMITH
Penwortham, Preston

Let's face it – I'm purrfect!
PETER WILKINSON
Guiseley, W Yorkshire

I love you
ROSEMARY BELL
Bourne, Lincolnshire

Sticking my neck out
BERYL KING
Rainham, Kent

facing page
Wise guy
JOHN LING
Haverhill, Suffolk

Doggin' around
BERT WHALLEY
Ulverston, Cumbria

Who me?
D COMPTON
Rendcomb, Gloucestershire

Save some for me
MRS SYLVIA WHALLEY
Ulverston, Cumbria

That's my flock!
ALLISON OWEN JONES
Cardiff

**What are you looking at
– I'm French you know**
KEVIN PERT
Staplehurst, Kent

Tasty
Miss Emily Horne
Crowborough, E Sussex

Misty and Sarah
Tony Perry
Gillingham, Dorset

Newly hatched swallowtail
PETER SMITH
Penwortham, Preston

Where is my dinner ?
PETER ROCCHICCIOLI
Hayling Island, Hampshire

Do I need a trim?
MR D A ALLCORN
Penzance, Cornwall

**So how would you
keep the rain off?**
MR & MRS B JACKSON
Silverdale, Staffordshire

Hurry up, take the picture
BRIAN HUGHES
St Helens, Merseyside

The dangerous brothers
MR A L DOUGLAS
Long Eaton, Nottinghamshire

Me and my shadow
DEBORAH PREECE
Crewe, Cheshire

**Don't look at us,
how about them!**
MR CHRISTOPHER POTTS
Launceston, Cornwall

Keep Britain tiny
BETH HUNTER
Sale, Cheshire

I wish we could go to the park
GILLY MANFORD
London SW4

**Shire horse display
– country show**
FIONA BARLTROP
Burgess Hill, W Sussex

My favourite spot
MRS L A HEDLEY
Bedford

Road rage

Mr E A F Goodyer mbe

Dartford, Kent

Wheel bow wow!
Mrs Judith Barnard
Derrythorpe, N Lincolnshire

**I'm sure I buried
that bone here**
Mr J E Bailey
Chelmsford, Essex

Where's that cat?
Mrs J Penk
Halesowen, W Midlands

**Ollie and Paul take
a nap together. Taken by a
blind man's sighted wife.**
Mrs G P Brookes
Redditch, Worcestershire

The Milky Bar kit
MRS K LODY
Horsell, Woking

**I'm supposed to find
this amusing!**
MRS J ROSSLEY
Alton, Hampshire

High spirits
R Spencer
Gillingham, Dorset

Heart of a swan's kiss
K Christie-Sturges
Sanderstead, Surrey

One man and his dogs
Mr S Wilkinson
Dudley, Worcestershire

Sporting friends
A. Yorke
Rhosgadfn, Gwynedd

Me and my shadow
MISS L RYAN
Abington, Northamptonshire

Give us a kiss, then
MALCOLM KUS
Willenhall, W Midlands

Togetherness
MALCOLM KUS
Willenhall, W Midlands

Innocence
M UNDERWOOD
Delapre, Northampton

Long road home
BILL ALLEN
Eastbourne, E Sussex

SECTION WINNER

I'll suffer for this tomorrow

HARRY SMITH

Westcliff on Sea, Essex

Sporting **Britain**

CHAPTER SEVEN

Turning on the style
Mike Wood
Tetbury, Gloucestershire

A quick 69!!!
Andrew Gibb
Perth

Goal hungry
Jackie E McCormick
Marske by Sea, Cleveland

Previous page
Collage
N Carter
London

**Women with balls - heading for
the goal of equal opportunities**
Claire Dutton
*Newcastle under Lyme,
Staffordshire*

Ooh Aah - mind my car!
Tim Hoy
Willesden, London

Under the shower
Mrs J A Shirley
Doncaster, South Yorkshire

It's not for the want of trying
Mrs C M Prince
Bournemouth, Dorset

Stumped
BILL McLEOD
Londonderry

Cricket tea
SIMON J GIBSON
Newmarket

Catch of the day
M Smith
Sheerness, Kent

Tackling up
Bert Whalley
Ulverston, Cumbria

**David (Lionheart) Holding,
a London marathon
paraplegic champion**
ERIC W GOODCHILD
Corby, Northamptonshire

**The warm up before
the Race for Life**
ANNABEL GRIFFIN
Kippen, by Stirling

The Red Hose, the
oldest continuously held
race in Scotland.
JIM BROWN
Livingston, West Lothian

Which way now?
DAVID CLEETON-WATKINS
Bwlch, Brecon

Come on Tim!
CHRIS BROWN
Burton on Trent, Staffordshire

Game, set, match: the weather
MARGARET MILLS
Newport, Gwent

Polo at Windsor
MIKE ROBERTS
Greenford, Middlesex

Us next
KEVIN JAQUISS
Baudon

Yacht race on the river Tay
DAVID ALEXANDER BARRIE
Dundee, Scotland

Fore sail
MR P NEWTON
Colchester, Essex

Blowing past (Henley)
CLIVE B HARRISON
Bracknell, Berkshire

Rapid power
MR MICHAEL RILEY
Gotham, Nottinghamshire

Facing page

Exhausted and going nowhere

Miss S Douglas

Thame, Oxon

The final hurdle

Mr T Rack

Northampton

Football - through closed eyelids

Joanna C Matthews

Altrincham, Cheshire

SECTION WINNER

That's the way to do it!

Mrs J Comley

Dorchester

Young **Britain**

CHAPTER EIGHT

Phoebe
MAISIE HILL
Lyme Regis, Dorset

I wonder...
PETER HAMILTON
Leytonstone, E. London

What a giggle
Mrs B Ferguson
Leicester

Miss Bubbles 1996
Lynda Key
Whitestone, Nuneaton

Ebony-Rae winning through
Mrs P R Davies
Caerphilly, Mid Glamorgan

**Smile please, it's hard work
being a photographer**
Jim Brown
Livingston, West Lothian

Breaching Hastings
KATHY SOUTHWELL
Edinburgh

**Grand-daughter playing
with water**
MR J GORNALL
Bicester, Oxon

**Birthday boy
Matthew King celebrates
his first birthday with
grandma,**
MR D COOPER
Blackpool, Lancashire

Young love at Butlins
ANON

It started with a kiss
ANDREW COOPER
Barrow-in-Furness, Cumbria

Close up

A VONRANKEN

Southend on Sea, Essex

Daisy dreamer
BARBARA ANN DOYLE
Conwy, North Wales

I can see you
MRS K CHRISTIE-STURGES
Sanderstead, Surrey

Pride in my country
NORMAN PASCOE
Firkby-in-Furness, Cumbria

Posting a letter
KAREN HARRISON
London

Excuse me while I concentrate
Ms S Foreman
King's Lynn, Norfolk

Is anyone looking?
Mandy Brooks
Cambridge

I like to get into a good book!
MRS JUDITH BARNARD
Scunthorpe, North Lincolnshire

Child bride
GARRY S MENZIES
East Linton, East Lothian

I see no ships
Mrs G Bellamy
Mellis, Suffolk

Jasmin - sand engineer.
Jasmin, 2 years and 4 months,
has a serious heart abnormality
Phil Whittaker
Hampton, Middlesex

Feeding time in silhouette
Mr T Rack
Northampton

The best of friends
HARRY SMITH
Westcliff on Sea, Essex

**What do you want to do
when you grow up?**
JULIA LLOYD-PARKS
Twyford, Berkshire

Emma and Fudge, her very own pony
ANON

From one kid to another
PATRICK KESTERTON
Ashby-de-la-Zouch, Leicestershire

Lots of fun
MRS Z KING
Tunbridge Wells, Kent

**Young Morris dancers
between performances**
Mrs P B Roberts
Downham Market, Norfolk

Why can't I come too ?
Malcolm Kus
Willenhall, West Midlands

Small supporter
F A HOWLETT
Stratford upon Avon, Warwickshire

**Who said I couldn't
feed myself?**
MRS J A DAVIS
Orpington, Kent

Happy birthday
CHRIS ROWE
Oxley, Wolverhampton

Lion-heart
MR P NEWTON
Colchester, Essex

Duck's swimming lesson
N.A.De-Pulford
Totnes, Devon

Swingin' Sara
Mr D W Harkness
Knutsford, Cheshire

Jacob's on the ball.
Two-year-old Jacob
Bonnett is a Royal
Brompton hole-in-
the-heart patient

THE TIMES

We all love a cuddle
MRS K CHRISTIE-STURGES
Sanderstead, Surrey

Dinner Time
MRS D HARVEY
Tilbury, Essex

Success
MRS AVRIL J LYNCH
Standish, Wigan

I like driving in Pat's car
STEVE CULSHAW
Portsmouth, Hampshire

**80 years of Cub Scouting
1916-1996**
M PULLEN
Shrewsbury

Three friends
JOANNA POPE
Clifton, Bristol

Look what we did
VANESSA KEELER
Hereford

Off duty choristers,
St John's College, Cambridge
Mrs Sue Rulliere
Cambridge

Young driver of the year
Christina Radmall
Shoreham, West Sussex

Off duty choristers,
St John's College, Cambridge
Mrs Sue Rulliere
Cambridge

Young driver of the year
Christina Radmall
Shoreham, West Sussex

**Nowhere to go,
nothing to do!**
ZOE WILSON
Perivale, Middlesex

**Lisa regrets her recent
shopping binge**
RACHAEL JONES
Aldridge, West Midlands

Higher state of conciousness
VICKI COUCHMAN
Southsea

Heart-breakers
RICHARD COOKE
Chichester, W. Sussex

Rollerblade for Britain
MARION DAVIES
London

Overleaf
Will Dad ring the bell?
CLIVE B HARRISON
Bracknell, Berkshire

SECTION WINNER

Smile, you're on candid camera
RACHEL BAYLIE
Lincoln

Tomorrow's Britain

CHAPTER NINE

Worzel Gummidge - 2000
REV GORDON STEER
Lingfied, Surrey

Here today, gone tomorrow?
ANGELA ROWLANDS
Launceston, Cornwall

Wot?
MR W J PRIESTMAN
Camberley, Surrey

Visitor - AD 2000?
Mr D L Harding
Tredegar, Gwent

Boot-e-full
Mrs J A Davis
Orpington, Kent

**When are you
going to be King?**
RICHARD COOKE
Chichester, Sussex

Contemplating the future
KATHY SOUTHWELL
Edinburgh

Blasting for new Cable TV
D AND A SNOWSELL
Upminster, Essex

Convenience Food
DOROTHY BULLIMORE
Farnham, Surrey

Like father, like son
Mrs C E Lougher-Harris
Bridgend, Mid-Glamorgan

**Photovoltaic cells at
Machynlleth, Wales**
Vanessa Keeler
Hereford

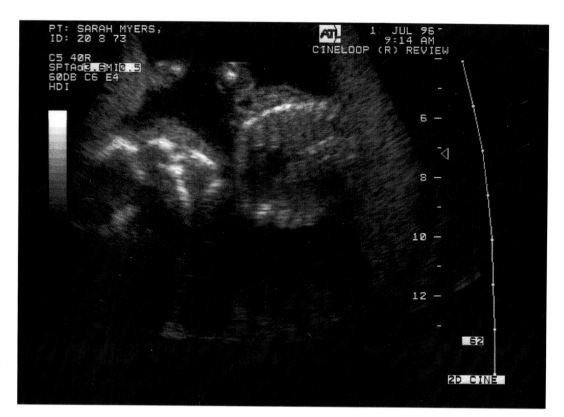

**My grandson or
grand-daughter, expected
November 1996**
<small>SUBMITTED BY SARAH MYERS</small>

New grandson
<small>MRS I F STONE</small>
Eastleigh, Hampshire

I do
CHRIS ROWE
Oxley, Wolverhampton

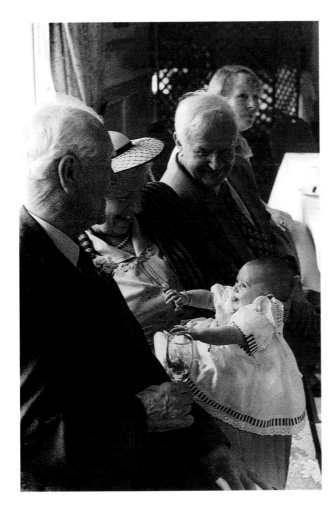

The welcoming committee
LINDSAY OLIVER
Pocklington, York

Saints preserve us!
CHRIS BROWN
Burton on Trent, Staffordshire

Mobile phone booth
STEVE GLADDEN
Crewe

Five hours to do my hair!
TONY SWIFT
Allestree, Derbyshire

**Our children have a bright
future at their fingertips**
Mrs E Hobbs
Plumstead, London

The new age
Richard Cooke
Chichester, W. Sussex

There'll always be an England
Mrs C M Prince
Bournemouth, Dorset

The Heart of the Heart of Britain

C H A P T E R   T E N

THE CERNE ABBAS GIANT IS GIVEN A HEART

MIKE MALONEY

A GIANT SEND-OFF

The Heart of Britain Campaign grabbed the headlines with a remarkable achievement on June 21, when hundreds of schoolchildren helped re-create the Cerne Abbas Giant, normally seen on a West Country hillside, in the heart of London – at Kenwood on Hampstead Heath.

Celebrities such as Warren Mitchell (right, who took the picture below) and Jeremy Beadle (far right) were on hand to make sure the event received the best possible coverage.

The highlight of the day came when the Giant was given a living heart – the Heart of Britain symbol created by a hundred children.

The striking moment was captured by Press and TV reporters circling overhead in a helicopter. Thanks to a giant effort by all concerned, the Heart of Britain campaign was off to a flying start.

Royal Brompton patients Darius Wyke-Little, Candice Mahoney, Jamie Poore, Jeremie Dallsingh, Abubakar Isa Othman, Alistair Beament, Caitlin Hines, Scott Rhodes, James Perry, Ross Ellis, Jessica Waugh, Danielle Stephenson, Emma Crampton, Angela Pridham, Emily Colgan and Frances Osakue with the Princess.

Jane Asher makes a special cake

Actress and cake shop owner Jane Asher baked a Heart of Britain cake for the Brompton children to give to Princess Diana on her 35th birthday – July 1.

DIANA AND THE HEART CHILDREN

On July 1, the start of Heart of Britain Week, these moving pictures appeared in a special edition the Daily Mirror. Taken by photographer Kent Gavin, they show the Princess on a visit to Royal Brompton's youngest heart and lung patients.

The Princess is a regular visitor, and all the children love her informal, friendly manner.

She is moved beyond words by the bravery of small children who have to fight such serious illness so early in their lives.

DAILY MIRROR — Heart of Britain

TAKE A PICTURE AND SAVE A LIFE

HEART OF BRITAIN is the charity campaign...

Ham&High

Police quiz Scout leader on assault

44-year-old suspended after claims of indecent attacks on two boys

By Alan Jones

Giant loses manhood — but gains a heart

ONE thousand children lined up to recreate the prehistoric chalk image of the Cerne Abbas giant in almost all his glory in the garden of the Kenwood House in Hampstead on Friday.

SCOTLAND'S CHAMPION — Daily Record

July 4, 1996

SINGALAWN: Wimbers goes pop

Volley good show from Sir Cliff!

By TRACEY HARRISON

VETERAN pop star Sir Cliff Richard made a racquet at soggy Wimbledon yesterday.

Record's big lift - just in time for T

KIND-HEARTED Record readers have given disabled pop fans a real lift after fears that they would miss T In The Park.

Backwards

See me, feel me, heal me!

VETERAN rocker Roger Daltrey...

DI-LIGHT Princess Diana's warmth and compassion show that she is Queen of Hearts Picture: KENT

HEART OF BRITAIN – THE B... FIND OUT WHAT MAKES

PATRICIA CORNWELL

'Grippingly tense'
The Times

FROM...

DAILY MIRROR EXCLUSIVE

MANIAC STALKS GIRL AGED 10

A STALKER who takes secret photos of a 10-year-old girl neighbour is expected today. Pervert Stewart Horseman, 36, has sneaked dozens of snaps of...

THREAT: Horseman

Full story – Pages 4 & 5

DAILY MIRROR

Tuesday, July 2, 1996

HONESTY, QUALITY, EXCELLENCE   30p

He's young, handsome, a winner.. and unlike Gazza he's single, girls

TIMBO

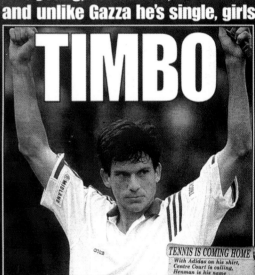

WINNER: Tennis sensation Timbo Henman celebrates his historic Wimbledon victory

By TRACEY HARRISON

TENNIS hunk Tim Henman became Britain's newest heart-throb last night after storming into the Wimbledon quarter-finals.

On the day Gazza married girlfriend Sheryl Failes, hunky Tim won through with a stunning Centre Court performance.

And after England's shattering semi-final defeat in Euro 96 he is now carrying the country's sporting hopes on his shoulders.

The 21-year-old raised his hand in a victory salute as he became the first British man to reach Wimbledon's last eight since 1973 – two years before he was born.

Adoring girl fans dubbed him Timbo and sang Tennis Is Coming Home – their version of the England soccer team's anthem.

He said later: "There's better tennis to come. I'm learning all the time. I'm only 21."

Odds on Timbo winning Wimbledon shortened to 16-1 last night – he began the tournament as a 100-1 outsider. The young Brit, ranked 62 in the world, took the Swede to beat

Turn to Page 2

TENNIS IS COMING HOME
With Adidas on his shirt,
Centre Court is calling,
Henman is his name
All the seeds are falling
'cos I remember when
Perry was best
And he outshone the rest
Roger Taylor got near
And Ginny waving
With three stripes on his shirt
The challenge cup is gleaming
Sixty years of hurt
Has never stopped us dreaming
It's coming home!
It's coming home!
Timbo's bringing tennis home.

COMING THIS WEEK

£2,000 EVERY WEEK FOR 10 YEARS TAX FREE
COLLECT TOKENS: SEE PAGE 11

INSIDE TODAY

TAKE A PHOTO.. SAVE A LIFE
4-PAGE GUIDE to Heart of Britain photograph appeal

DAILY MIRROR

Monday, July 8, 1996

HONESTY, QUALITY, EXCELLENCE   30p

£2,000 EVERY WEEK FOR 10 YEARS TAX FREE
Token 4: SEE PAGE 13

17 kiddies hit by poison seaside virus

EXCLUSIVE

By PETER KANE and JEREMY ARMSTRONG

SEVENTEEN children have been struck down by a crippling virus after going paddling on the same stretch of beach.

The youngsters – aged from five to 14 – have been left in agony, unable to walk, and suffering bouts of uncontrollable bleeding.

Experts fear they are victims of a virus linked to polluted sea water at Harwich, Essex.

Action

The Government faced demands for urgent action.

WHAT AN ACE: Finalists Krajicek and Washington grin in delight as daring Melissa streaks across Wimbledon Centre Court yesterday Picture: ARNOLD SLATER

GAME, SET AND FLASH

First streaker at Wimbledon

By TRACEY HARRISON

THIS was the moment cheeky Melissa Johnson became Wimbledon's first streaker.

Wearing nothing but a tiny pinafore Melissa, 23, gave a full display flash as the Centre Court finalists Richard Krajicek and MaliVai Washington grinned in delight. Pals of Melissa, who was arrested, said: "She's a fruitcake."

See Pages 2 & 3

Turn to Page 5

THE TIMES SATURDAY JUNE 22 1996

Owner of house in road rage hunt admits Noye link

By ADRIAN LEE and JOANNA BALE

THE owner of a house which is linked to the "road rage" killing of Stephen Cameron admitted yesterday that he knew Kenneth Noye, the Brink's-Mat robber, whom police want to trace.

Noye: police in M25 case want to speak to him

A thousand children recreating the giant at Kenwood House

ROYAL EXCLUSIVE ON DIANA'S PLEA FOR THE HEART CHILDREN

'They are so tiny, so sick, so vulnerable'

TAKE A PHOTO .. SAVE A LIFE

DAILY Mirror

ROYAL EXCLUSIVE
Princess Diana backs our Heart of Britain appeal

Monday, July 1, 1996   HONESTY, QUALITY, EXCELLENCE   30p

MY BRAVE FRIENDS: Princess Diana at the Royal Brompton Hospital. The children were thrilled by her visit. And Diana was delighted to support an appeal which will save the lives of more of Britain's young heart victims   Picture: KENT GAVIN, Royal Photographer of the Year

DIANA AND THE HEART CHILDREN

Have a heart.

Take a picture.

What does the Heart of Britain mean to you? Take a photo this week and it could live forever as one of 300 chosen by our celebrity judges to appear in the 'Heart of Britain' book.

There are nine categories, which might give you some ideas: Young Britain, Caring Britain, Animal Britain, Britain on the Move, Sporting Britain, Good Time Britain, Beautiful Britain, Working Britain and Tomorrow's Britain.

The picture judged best in each category wins an Olympus Mju-1 compact camera.

Send us your three best photographs, together with a £2 donation and entry form, available from BP garages, Dillons, Dixons, John Menzies, WH Smith, Waterstone's, Mirror Group Newspapers or by telephoning 0891 252605.

Heart of Britain

July 1st-7th

In support of Royal Brompton Hospital, the leading edge in heart resea
Supported by: AMV Group · Bookman Projects · Dixons · Halifax Building Society · Hillsdown Holdings · Love T

How Heart of Britain Week looked in the Press

Below, Daily Mirror Editor Piers Morgan with the front page of his newspaper for the 1st of July – the start of Heart of Britain Week.

Picture: Chris Grieve

Org jolly giant with a big new heart

By ROBIN YOUNG

Snapping Back

Heart of Britain Week saw some crazy stunts as the nation's photographers strove to bring us the unusual, the perplexing, the bizarre. This anonymous contributor clearly wanted to get his own back on the speed cameras that are now such a feature of motoring in Britain.

A Dunking at Henley

A hawk-eyed photographer was looking hard for his Heart of Britain picture at Henley Regatta. As he walked along the rain-lashed banks of the Thames on Friday, July 5, he saw the picture opportunity of a lifetime. A young lady, with too much to drink, toppled slowly backwards... Quick as a flash, his camera started clicking to produce this unique set of pictures.

Sure, accidents do happen. But when they happen to newspaper photographer Mike Maloney, you wonder. Never mind. Mike always has an eye for a front page picture. And when it's all in a good cause – publicity for the Heart of Britain campaign – we turn a blind eye when we see Maloney tip the sodden girl a tenner for her trouble.

The girl in the drink? Sabine Khan. "It's actually warmer in the water than out", said the game lass.

THE BOOKSELLER WINNER

Saturn on the Move
NEIL ADAMS
Balloch, Scotland

The Bookseller Magazine ran a Heart of Britain
photographic competition for its readers, which was
judged by Editor Louis Baum and reporter and
photography enthusiast Caroline Sylge. The
atmospheric photograph above was chosen as winner.

Daisy

DESMOND LYNAM

Mark Proud is in his early forties. He is married to Frances and the have a four-year-old son named Matthew. Mark is an ordinary bloke, more kind and caring than most, perhaps, and a good father. He is also blind – he lost his sight in early childhood.

Mark tries to lead a normal life, including playing with Matthew and teaching him about the world. And for Heart of Britain week Mark decided to take a picture of the son he can't see, using an automatic camera.

"Taking a photo of my son proves that I am the same as any other man. " said Mark. " Of course I find it sad that I will never be able to see the results of my photography, but I hope the pictures will give pleasure to others."

Adam Faith is one of Heart of Britain's most enthusiastic supporters.

Adam knows from personal experience the importance of heart research – 10 years ago he had a bypass operation.

He says: "I was lucky. I had surgery and have been fine ever since. But who knows if I will need more in the future? That is why research and the Heart of Britain campaign are so necessary."

Adam is pictured below with young heart patient Josh Wells, left, and his brother Mitchell.

Portrait photography chain Parasol got into the spirit of Heart of Britain by inviting their customers to send in their favourite portraits with a donation to the Appeal. The winner and three runners-up are shown here.

KARL & JESSICA JACKSON
Bury St Edmunds, Suffolk
Karl is a young heart patient

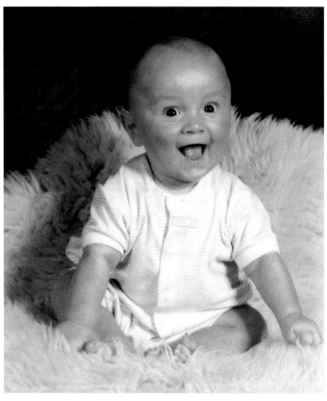

LUKE GRIFFITHS
Bishops Cleeve, Cheltenham, Gloucestershire

MATTHEW BRYANT
Llangunnor, Carmarthen

PARASOL PORTRAIT WINNER

ELLEN TAYLOR
New Cross, Manchester

Singer Jan Monroe has put her heart and soul into the campaign –
her version of Cilla Black's classic Anyone Who Had a Heart was
released to raise funds for the campaign. Pictured here with
Robson & Jerome and starmakers Mike Stock & Matt Aitken.

Anthea Turner says:

"I've always got a camera in my pocket and I photograph everything. I have a total record of every event that I go to, my work, in fact everything that is interesting is captured by my camera and everyone loves looking at my scrapbooks. They are full of the people that I have spoken to. I have a privileged job and it's good to have a record so that when I am old I can look back at my life."

Below, Anthea takes a picture of floor manager Siobhan O'Donnell and sound assistant Jane Holden on the set of GMTV.

Cool Cats with Cameras

The cast of the hit musical Cats came out to support Heart of Britain week. Keen photographers amongst the cast included David Malet, Alistair Bull, Nunzio Lombardo, Robert Yeal Samantha Biddulph, Katie Knight Adams, Rosemary Ford and Christian Storm.

Snooker star Steve Davis, one of the most active of the Heart of Britain Campaign's celebrity supporters, found himself in the mood for Christmas in the heart of the year.

The BBC were filming the Christmas Special of the Big Break programme, and Steve took a pot shot at John Parrot, Jim Davidson and Dennis Taylor.

Celebrity Britain took the campaign to its heart. On this page Nick Berry, star of Heartbeat, shows one of his favourite scenes. Arnold Peters and June Spencer – Jack and Peggy Woolley from the Archers – get busy with a Heart of Britain camera. And Liz Bradley and Peter Baldwin from Coronation Street toast the fundraising efforts.

On the page opposite, Frank Carson and Russ Abbott show off their Heart of Britain caps.

Newsreader Martyn Lewis is a keen photographer. "I prefer people to places; they are so much more interesting," he said. "I did a series some time ago on other newsreaders relaxing at home and that was a great assignment. I saw my colleagues in a totally different light."

Fellow newsreader Moira Stewart feels differently. "I hate having my photograph taken – but Martyn is a good friend and it helps to have someone you know take your photograph. You feel more relaxed."

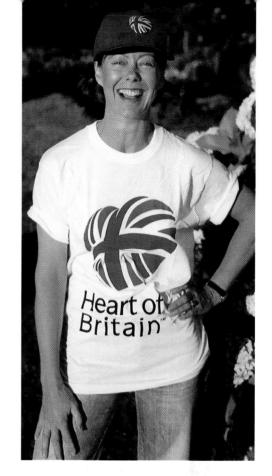

Pin-ups for Heart of Britain

Michael Ball
Petula Clark
Sarah Van Der Berg from Neighbours
Penny Smith and Jilly Johnson
Billy Murray and Mark Wingett, actors from The Bill
Jenny Agutter
Gavin Hastings

C ATEGORY - ?

Lee & Katharine Harper 28/3/81
taken by Lee's Brother - Brian
Happiness x2
Category - ?

Lee, Mark & Neil Harper
Lee & Neil's Birthday
17/11/1987
taken by Mammy
Category - ?
Happiness x3

Lee Harper
17/11/1937 - 5/4/92
Died of Heart Disease
Photo taken by
Mark Harper
aged 10 years

Sadness x A whole
multitude of
family, friends,
colleagues & neighbours

Category - ?

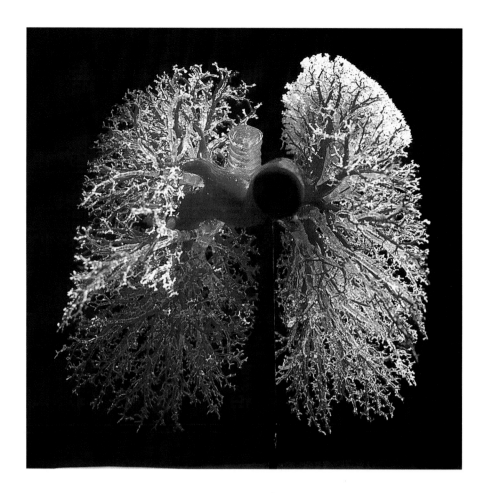

TREES OF LIFE

If only it could be shown, the most breathtaking picture in this book would be a picture that reveals all the branching and mingling streams of our blood circulation. As a whole, the circulation cannot be seen. But we can begin to glimpse what it must be like from this cast, which shows the branching forms of arteries and airways of the lungs. The resin cast was prepared for the Brompton Hospital over 30 years ago. The arteries are shown in red. Interwoven with them is the tree of airways which, throughout life, would have carried breath to and from the bloodstream.

To appreciate the complexity of the blood circulation, consider what is *not* shown by the cast: the smallest branches – intricate capillary networks, finer than hairs – have not been preserved. Nor has the tree of veins that would have carried oxygenated blood back from the lungs to the heart.

Between the lungs would be the heart, which propels two swirling, pulsing streams: from the body to the lungs, and from the lungs to the body. And the muscle of the heart itself has to be nourished through the branches of the coronary arteries and veins.

Then we have to consider all the surrounding, far-reaching parts of the circulation – the trees of arteries that spread throughout the body (head, limbs, trunk and organs) and their delicate webs of capillaries where blood seeps through the various tissues, before converging back through the veins.

Now bring that all to life – flowing and counter-flowing, pulsing and seeping. The various parts move simultaneously and in sequence. As blood circulates, it diverges outwards, giving and receiving in each tissue before returning to the centre. Very many streams converge to the veins that fill the heart. The heart responds tirelessly, propelling the blood on its way. The circulating blood sustains the diversity of our body . . . it maintains unity in complexity, and continuity through continual change.

Philip Kilner
British Heart Foundation Research Fellow at Royal Brompton Hospital

TREVOR LEIGHTON

Britain

As seen by the Professionals

CHAPTER ELEVEN

BRIAN ARIS

Shot for 'Vanity Fair' (Italy)

JOHN STODDART

Streaker Melissa Johnson at
Wimbledon, July 7, 1996
ANDY HOOPER

Lee Hurst
BRIAN MOODY

**Edinburgh, Salisbury Crags
below Arthur's seat**
David Corfield

Peter Bowles
MIKE MALONEY

Robert Powell
MIKE MALONEY

MARTYN MOORE

John Barnes
TERRY O'NEILL

Pastures Green
Liz Ball
Calderstones, Liverpool